The Story of Today

Today is a brand new story, one that's never been told before. It isn't a fairly tale, bedtime book, or beach read. It's an epic adventure ready to be lived. It's being written moment by moment, one breath at a time. Every word we share in conversation, every choice we make throughout the day, every hug we give, thought we ponder, and kindness we extend is etched into our very personal tale of today.

Although the book of our life is a work in progress, the chapter of today can't be edited once it's passed. That makes every moment all the more precious—as well as the need to be intentional, all the more vital. It's true that circumstances out of our control may push the plot of our lives in one direction or another, sometimes leading us toward a storyline we'd never choose on our own. Yet it isn't what happens to us, but how we respond to what happens that will determine whether our saga will ultimately be a tragedy, comedy, love story, or quest.

The good news is that this isn't a story we write alone. Our co-author is also our Creator. Before we were born, God wrote us into being, setting our life—and this day—in motion. Together we have the chance to write a story that's uniquely beautiful, one worth celebrating.

Working hand-in-hand with God, what will you do or say that will help compose a memorable, praiseworthy chapter today?

For the Lord
seeth not as man seeth;
for man looketh
on the outward
appearance,
but the
Lord
looketh on the
heart.

1 Samuel 16:7

Eye Priority

Our eyes are an amazing gift. They allow us to enjoy the brilliance of a sunset, the glisten of morning dew on a blade of grass, or the winsome smile of someone we love. But, when paired with the often critical nature of the human heart, our eyes can also lead us to make judgments that aren't based on truth.

For example, suppose a driver cuts you off in traffic. What you "see" may be an aggressive, entitled motorist, someone you have no interest in knowing personally. But what if you knew the rest of the story: the driver has just been notified there's been an accident and he's on his way to the hospital to see if his little boy is going to make it. If we could only see what's in that man's heart...fear, grief, anxiety, love...it would change how we see him as a person.

We make a lot of snap judgements with our eyes. Some of them reveal the state of our own hearts, including our personal prejudices, fears, and insecurities. What story does your heart tell you when you see someone who's homeless? Someone dressed to the nines? Someone of a different race or ethnicity? Someone who's physically or mentally challenged? What does your heart say when you look at yourself in the mirror?

God is the only one who can truly see "behind the scenes" all the way to the heart. But He can help us learn to look at others—and ourselves—through a lens of grace. It all begins with a simple prayer: Lord, please help me see the world through Your eyes. What a wonderful way to start the day!

Be still,
and know
that
I am God.

Psalm 46:10

Fast and Furious...or Quiet and Curious

Life is loud...phones ringing, babies crying, cars speeding, televisions blaring. In the midst of all that noise, we're usually moving as fast as we can, trying to make it to an appointment on time, get dinner on the table, or beat a deadline. No wonder we're so tired at the end of the day.

When our normal pace is fast and furious, it's easy to lose sight of the things that don't demand our attention. That includes God. He doesn't shout or push His way into our lives. He waits. He whispers. He beckons us with His constant love. But unless we slow down long enough to breathe, quiet our own inner monologue, and listen patiently for His still, small voice, it's easy to forget He's even there. We may forget Him, but He never forgets us. That assurance is exactly what we need when life feels out of control.

When we're quiet long enough to ponder what it means to "know that I am God," we'll be reminded that we are not. We're not in control of this world. But we know, and are known, by the One who is. The more we learn to trust and depend on Him, the less pressure we'll feel to keep all of the plates of our lives spinning frantically at the same time. We may even realize that we can set a few of those plates down, if not permanently, at least long enough to rest.

Crazy days happen. But when they do, God offers us a place of peace and renewal smack dab in the middle of the chaos. All we need to do is stop, breathe, and remember who He is—and who we are to Him.

I THANK
MY
God
UPON
EVERY
remembrance
OF
you.

Philippians 1:3

The Gift of Gratitude

There are people in our lives who can make us smile just by thinking of them. Who's on your list? A sibling, child, grandchild, or spouse? A parent who's grown into a friend? A confidante who's stood beside you through good times and bad, laughter and tears, for more years than either one of you'd care to admit? Perhaps it's someone who's headed home to heaven before you.

Those we love are often on our mind. They remain close at heart, regardless of how many miles or years may separate us. Not only is every person we cherish, but every memory we share, a priceless gift. Gifts like that deserve a thank you note.

It only takes a few moments of our time to let someone we love know how much they mean to us. Social media, text, and email help us keep in touch more easily than we could a generation ago. However, an actual phone call, an unexpected card in the mailbox, or a gift sent simply to say, "You're on my mind," adds a depth of sincerity to our sentiment—as does simply saying the words "Thank you" and "I love you" aloud.

And we know
that all things work together
for good to them that love

GOD,

to them who are the called
according to his purpose.

Romans 8:28

The Raw Material of Life

It's easy to view life as a series of good days and bad days, dividing what's helpful from what's hurtful, the pleasant from the painful. But what if there was a seed of something good planted in everything that happens? Thanks to God's love and power, there is.

That doesn't mean everything that happens is good. It also doesn't mean we put on an oversized pair of rose-colored glasses and pretend to see the world in a more favorable light than is honest or true. But as we lean on God through the ups and downs of life, He changes our perspective to more accurately reflect His own. He enables us to see those seeds of good take root and grow. Maybe not right away. But farther down the road, as we look back on our lives, we can see where God's hand was at work, even on our darkest of days.

We see how attributes like patience, perseverance, and courage grew in what seemed like the foulest of soils. We note the now-cherished friends we met on a road we never would have chosen to take. We recognize that some of the blessings we celebrate today are actually sweeter because hard times taught us how truly precious they are. We begin to understand how God took our brokenness and reconfigured it into a mosaic of surprising beauty.

With God's perspective, power, and purpose at work in our lives, everything we experience is raw material. It all holds the potential to be transformed into something good.

...the fruit
of the
Spirit is love, joy,
peace, forbearance,
kindness, goodness,
faithfulness,
gentleness
and
self-control.

Galatians 5:22-23 NIV

Bountiful Harvest

Let's talk fruit. We know the basics. Fruit grows on trees, bushes, or vines. It's not only part of a balanced diet, it's tasty—as long as it's eaten when it's ripe. Pick it too early and it's hard and bitter. Let it ripen too long and it falls to the ground, wasted, and equally inedible.

The same can be said of spiritual fruit. We can't grow it ourselves through our own talent or hard work. In John 15:5, Jesus says, "I am the vine; ye are the branches." As long as we stay connected to God, fruit will naturally grow over time, maturing when the season is right. But God didn't create fruit just to hang out on the branch and look good. He designed it to nourish people. He offers us that same opportunity.

Certainly, our own lives feel healthier and happier when qualities such as goodness, kindness, and self-control are growing in our hearts. But unless we're sharing that fruit with others, we're wasting part of the harvest. It's like letting it rot on the vine. The more we reach out to others with the gifts God is working in and through us, the more fruit our heart will yield.

Chances are there will be times when our own inattentiveness or selfishness may cause a subpar harvest. Spiritual fruit, like literal "garden variety" fruit, needs attention throughout the year to help it produce a plentiful crop. So, when we find our self-control lacking, our joy waning, or our love falling short, instead of criticizing ourselves, let's ask God for a fruit inspection. If our fruit isn't as hardy as we would hope, perhaps it's time to draw even closer to the vine, and allow God to do a bit of pruning in our lives.

I WILL PRAISE THEE;
FOR I AM *fearfully*
AND
wonderfully
MADE.

PSALM 139:14

Miracle in the Making

As you're reading this book, your heart is beating, your blood's circulating, your eyes are focusing, your digestive system is turning your last meal into fuel, your medulla oblongata is keeping you breathing, and your mind is pondering—or wandering—depending on how much you wish you were taking a nap right now. And that's just the tip of the anatomical iceberg. Talk about multi-tasking!

God's creation of each one of us is truly wonderful and awe-inspiring (the word "fearful" in the Bible is synonymous with "awesome"). Furthermore, every person since the dawn of time is unique. Yes, we may share some of the same general physical characteristics, such as having a nose or a belly button. But our fingerprints, our DNA, the way we think and talk and interact with the world is all a one-of-a-kind, only once-in-all-of-time, package deal. Just thinking about the complexity and possibility God has woven into each individual is enough to make our cerebrum hum with activity.

It should also be more than enough to spur us on toward praise. Praise means to applaud, express admiration, compliment, honor or give thanks. God deserves every one of those accolades and so much more. Today, why not take a few moments to consider the phenomenal way God fashioned the masterpiece called "you"? Then, freely offer Him the gift of praise. Praise God through song, prayer, art, writing in your journal...whatever way your heart is most comfortable expressing gratitude and awe. Like a handmade gift given to a parent by his or her child, your gift of praise will be treasured by the One who made you with such creativity and care.

Let Us
LOVE
ONE
Another
1 JOHN 4:7

We Are Family

These are the words of Jesus. Brief, yet to the point. In essence, He's saying, "We're all family, so let's act like it." But we all know how families often interact—especially young siblings. As parents we're constantly reminding our kids to share, apologize, take turns, be gentle, use kind words, and forgive. It can be frustrating at imes to repeat ourselves over and over, but we know that self-centeredness takes a while to outgrow. Unfortunately, some of us never do.

Age doesn't automatically equal maturity. Time and experience can certainly help us grow up, but selfishness clings to us like a static-filled sock to a pair of freshly laundered trousers. We need God's help to break that attraction. The more we allow God to work in our lives, the more our love will begin to resemble that of Jesus.

But that doesn't happen without us spending some time "parenting" ourselves. Every evening before going to bed, look back over your day. Consider your interactions with others. Where did you love well? Where did you fall short? Do you need to improve how you share, apologize, take turns, be gentle, use kind words, or forgive? Ask God to give you the opportunity to practice those skills the next day.

As God's children, we're all growing and maturing together. Jesus is the only one who has love fully mastered. Let's look to Him as our example—and learn to do more than just "play nice." Let's be willing to learn how to love those around us faithfully, authentically, and sacrificially.

CALL UNTO ME, AND I WILL ANSWER THEE.

Jeremiah 33:3

On Call

Have you ever prayed about something and felt like you were receiving a heavenly busy signal? In this modern world of email, text, and instant messaging, having to wait for a response for any length of time feels like an imposition. We're accustomed to getting what we want when we want it. If we have a question, a search engine can answer it. If we need a special ingredient for a recipe, we can order it online and have it at our door by dinner. If we have a prayer that weighs heavy on our heart, surely God can deliver more quickly than the pizza place down the road!

When it comes to prayer, we have a dedicated line straight to God available 24 hours a day. But that doesn't mean God is waiting to take our order. He's our loving Father, not our delivery boy. With God, "fast" isn't as important as "best."

God longs to respond to His children's needs. But like any good parent, He knows better than his children do when it comes to providing what is most helpful and appropriate at this time in their lives. Just because we don't see the answer we've pictured in our minds to a prayer we've faithfully prayed doesn't mean God isn't listening. His answer may be "no" or "not now." It may also be that His answer arrives in such a totally unexpected way that we absolutely miss it.

In the end, prayer is part communication, part mystery. Even if we don't fully understand how it works, let's continue to call and in faith, trust God will answer in His own time and His own way.

I AM COME
THAT THEY MIGHT
HAVE LIFE,
AND THAT THEY MIGHT
HAVE IT
MORE
abundantly.

JOHN 10:10

More Can Be Beautiful

The word "abundance" easily brings to mind images that resemble a child's view of Christmas...presents piled high, our every want, need, and whim not only met, but exceeded. But an abundant life isn't the same as a privileged life. It doesn't guarantee we'll move into our dream house, our pantry will overflow with gourmet food, and we'll live happily ever after.

An abundant life is a rich life, but not necessarily in the monetary sense. It's filled with treasures that are stored in the heart, instead of clutched in our hands. Yes, we may receive some lovely material blessings along the way. However, an abundant life is characterized more by a deep sense of contentment with what we already have, than by a garage filled to overflowing with stuff.

An abundant life offers us things that money can't buy, riches that can't be lost, stolen, or broken. Receiving life "more abundantly" means more peace, more love, more grace, more gratitude, and more of life itself—an eternal life that extends beyond the boundary of death. A full life can be a simple life, even an austere one, yet it overflows over with joy, purpose, and unconditional love.

So, when you're asked to count your blessings, don't stop with those you can see with your eyes. Look deeper. Consider how knowing God has changed your life for the better. Consider how it's changed you as a person, as a friend, a parent, a spouse, a servant to those in need. Consider how it's filled your heart with riches beyond measure.

With God all things are possible.

Matthew 19:26

Expect the Unexpected

A world created from nothing. Lazarus being raised from the dead. The Red Sea parting, a donkey talking, and water being changed into wine. In the Bible, we read about so many miraculous events taking place, all attributed to God's almighty hand. Do miracles like these still take place today? People of faith can't seem to agree.

Yet God continues to forgive what seems unforgivable. He brings good out of circumstances we deem horrible. He accepts us with a love that's unconditional. He changes our heart in ways that, through our own will power, were unattainable. He fills our lives with blessings, strength, and hope that we once may have deemed unimaginable. Yes, miracles still happen. And with God, we can continue to expect the unexpected.

So, don't be afraid to pray for what seems impossible. God's still in the business of surprising us with answers to questions we haven't even thought yet to ask.

In everything give thanks...

1 Thessalonians 5:18

The Gift That Keeps On Giving

Saying "thank you" is considered common courtesy. If someone holds the door for us, delivers a pizza, or fixes a flat tire, it's simply good form to voice our gratitude. But expressing our thanks, for blessings big and small, does more than showcase good manners. It actually perpetuates a cycle of thankfulness and good will.

Recent research shows that expressing our heartfelt thanks verbally, or writing a note or offering a small token of our appreciation, leaves us feeling more grateful and less depressed for a prolonged period afterwards. Not only that, it does the same for the person who receives our recognition. That's a cycle worth perpetuating!

It appears the more we get in the habit of showing our appreciation, the more grateful we'll feel about everything. No wonder God encourages us to give thanks. Whether we're praising Him for what He's doing in our lives, acknowledging the blessings we've received in a blessings journal, or expressing our gratitude to those God has brought into our lives, giving thanks is as much of a gift to ourselves as it is to those we're thankful for.

GOD IS OUR
REFUGE
AND
STRENGTH,
A VERY PRESENT HELP
IN TROUBLE.
Psalm 46:1

Safe Haven

A car feels like a pretty sturdy refuge in a storm. After all, the average vehicle weighs over 2 tons. Yet it only takes six inches of water before a driver can lose control. A foot of water, and vehicles will begin to float. Two feet of rushing water and most vehicles, including trucks and SUVs, will be carried away.

Regardless of the size of your current storm, God provides a safe haven that remains steadfast and secure. Best of all, it's just a prayer away. And that prayer can be as simple as a heartfelt, "Help!"

"Prayer" is the first of five Ps to remember when you're in need of rescue. Prayer immediately reminds you of God's "Presence." It reminds you that you're not alone in your troubles. God is near, even if you're struggling to see or feel Him in the midst of circumstantial chaos and confusion.

You can trust God is near, because of His "Promises." (That's "P" number three!) The more familiar you get with the Bible, the more God's Words will come to mind when you need comfort and reassurance. When you have the chance, turn to the Psalms (that's "P" number four) and begin reading to find solid footing. Anywhere will do. Read slowly and thoughtfully. You can even try reading aloud. Even though the circumstances may not be the same, people centuries ago turned to God in their troubles and found solace and safety. Their emotional and spiritual journeys are recorded there.

Finally, consider how God came through for them in the past. Then, call to mind any situations where God has done the same for you. ("Past" is the final "P.") Recalling God's faithfulness in the past, will help you find comfort and strength in the present.

Blessed Are
The Peacemakers:
For They Shall Be Called
The Children Of God.

Matthew 5:9

The Peace Process

It may be jokingly referred to as a beauty queen's "fondest wish," but world peace is far from a laughing matter. Every evening the nightly news fills our homes with eyewitness accounts of heartbreaking incidents that show this wish is far from coming true. Treaties, policies, sanctions, and military intervention can only go so far. What it really comes down to is the choices and actions of every individual. That includes each one of us.

Though our attempts to promote peace may be on a much smaller scale, every time we stop and listen instead of impulsively reacting, work harder to foster understanding than to win an argument, generously give more than our share, refuse to join the gossip mill, pray for our enemies (or simply those who rub us the wrong way) instead of talking behind their backs, apologize, forgive, and extend grace to every person who crosses our path (even the unreasonable ones), we take a step toward cultivating peace.

One of Jesus' "nicknames" is the Prince of Peace. We show we're related to Him when we do our part in not only maintaining, but being pro-active in the peace process, whether it's with our friends and family, our community, our country or even globally. We can start by allowing God's peace to make its home in our own heart. The more at peace we are inside ourselves, the easier it will be for reconciliation and grace to flow from us into the lives of those around us.

Every good gift
and every
perfect gift is from
above.

James 1:17

When Every Day is Christmas

Think about the best gifts you've ever received. Perhaps they were for Christmas or your birthday. Maybe they were a total surprise—given for no reason other than to let you know you were loved. What made those gifts so special? Were they exactly what you wanted or needed? Were they a perfect fit for your personality, your lifestyle or sense of fashion? Or maybe, what made these gifts so memorable was the fact that they demonstrated how very well someone knew you.

Who knows you better than the One who created you? Even before you took your first breath, God knew what you needed...and He still does. So, when He sends a gift your way, it's not only good, but perfect.

The only problem is that God is such a generous giver that it can be easy for us to take His gifts for granted. The food we eat, where we live, the people we love, the abilities we possess, the health and strength that powers us through another day...we're overloaded with good and perfect gifts. That's one reason why when some of the wonderful things we've been given are no longer available to us, we get a bit snippy. We've ceased to view them as gifts. Instead, we feel as though God owes them to us.

The more we nurture a habit of gratitude for what we've been given, the more we'll recognize and appreciate God's gifts, and the less we'll take them for granted. That means that when a few of our usual gifts are "missing" from today's line-up, we can still maintain a thankful heart. We can be grateful for what we have, freely ask God for what we need, then accept whatever does—and does not—come our way.

Do not be anxious
about anything,
but in every situation,
by prayer and petition,
with
thanksgiving,
present your
requests
to God.

Philippians 4:6 NIV

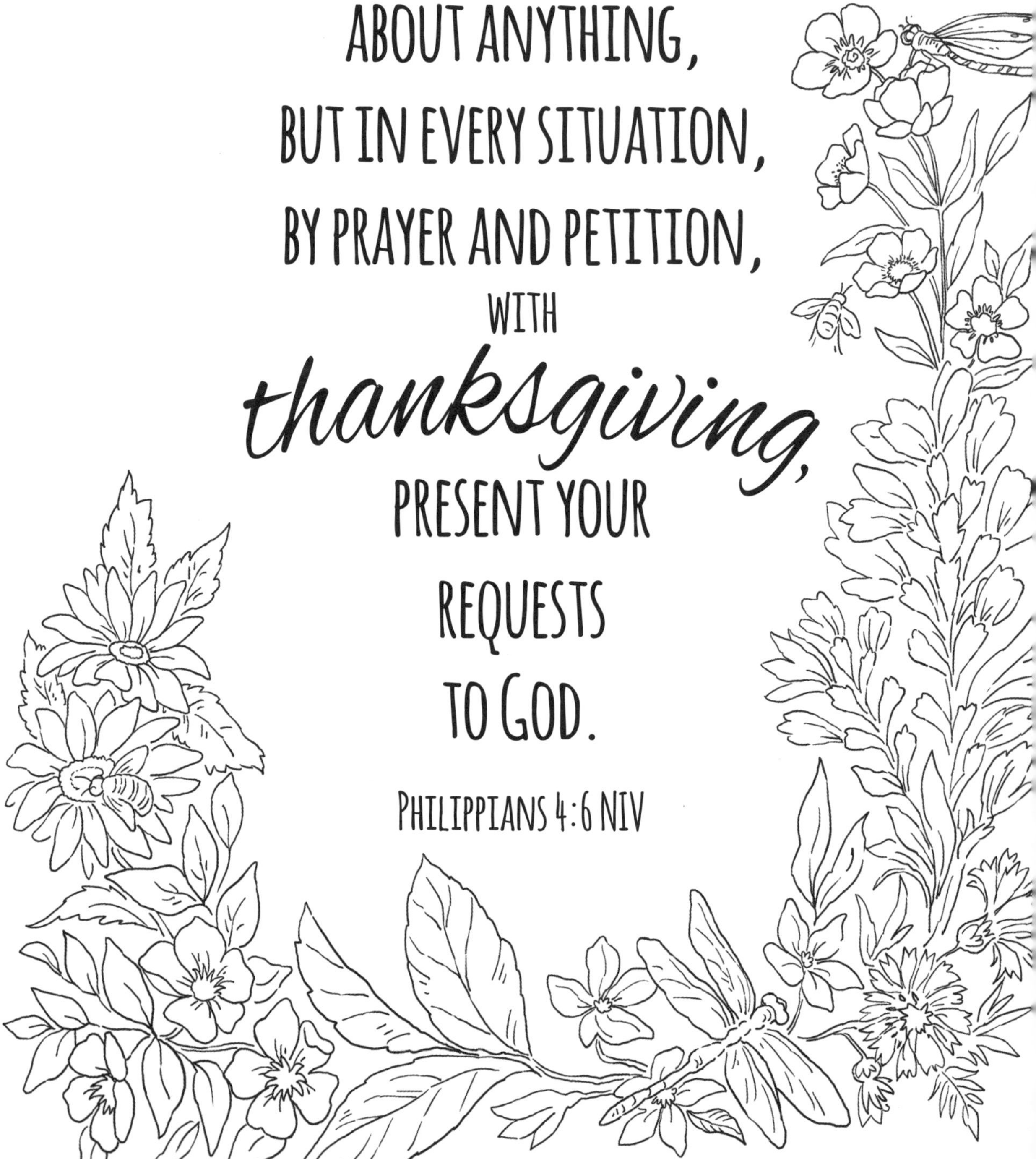

The Power of Prayer

Do you know why we blow out candles on our birthday? Because in Greece, centuries ago, it was believed that prayers drifted more quickly up to heaven on smoke than they could on good old regular air. Somewhere over time, prayers and wishes, along with birthdays and ordinary days, intertwined with tradition. Now, a birthday doesn't seem complete without candles on the cake. But how about prayer? Is it more of a tradition, like birthday candles, or a welcome part of our daily life?

Our prayers don't need smoke to facilitate their way into heaven. They also don't need to be uttered from a kneeling position, with our eyes closed, voiced in archaic or formal language, and saved for special occasions or a predetermined time. All prayers need, to reach the listening ear of our loving God, is sincerity of heart.

Prayer is appropriate, and effective, in any and every situation. When we're anxious, when worry, fear, anger, grief, or confusion threaten to displace God's peace and joy in our lives, prayer helps us regain balance and perspective. Through prayer, we can invite God's strength, wisdom and power to calm our heart and direct us in the way we should go. We can ask for help, as well as voice our questions and doubts, confess our love and our failures, and thank God that He hears us anytime, anywhere.

At its core, prayer is simply talking to God about whatever is on our heart. The more we get in the habit of sharing our concerns with God throughout the day, the more we'll be aware of His presence and power at work in our lives.

He that
walketh with
wise men
shall be
wise.

Proverbs 13:20

Be a Wise Guy

If you could have lunch with anyone in the world who would it be? Perhaps the more interesting question would be: Why? What makes that person so fascinating to you? Is it someone you look up to or admire? Someone you're dazzled by, like a superstar or newsmaker? Someone you feel is a kindred spirit, even though you may have never met?

What attracts us to a particular person tells us a lot about our own heart. It reveals what traits we hold in high regard. Although one lunch with someone may not change our life, hanging out with anyone for an extended period of time can influence our own character: for better or for worse. Why do you think parents are so concerned about the circle of friends their children choose to keep?

Our heavenly Father cares about the very same thing. He knows that those with whom we "walketh" (which is a biblical way of saying the people we "hang out" with) can actually help us grow wiser. It's like a "free gift with purchase." Not only do we gain the joy of relationship, we actually become more insightful and discerning when we walketh, talketh and hangeth out with those who are wise in God's eyes, instead of their own.

What wise guys and gals do you have by your side to encourage, challenge, and support you? Is there someone you admire, perhaps someone who's a bit farther down the road spiritually than you are now, with whom you'd like to become better acquainted? Treat that person to coffee and a chat. Walketh awhile together. You'll both be the wiser for it.

We are the clay,
and thou
our potter;
and we all
are the work
of thy hand.

Isaiah 64:8

Father Knows Best

Michelangelo had just finished his soon-to-be-famous statue of the David. Covered in marble dust, and weary from the difficult task, he turned toward home. Then the words, "Hey, Mike!" echoed through the empty studio. Incredulous, Michelangelo turned back to his masterpiece.

"No offense, but I think my arms are a bit too long," David critiqued his creator through cold marble lips. "Can you shorten them up a bit? And what's up with my hair? It looks like I haven't used any product since the Dark Ages! Most importantly, where are my clothes? Certainly I'm not going to go fight a giant au naturel?"

Never happened? Of course not. Works of art don't speak back to the one who created them. While it's true that artwork is usually inanimate, and that God fashioned us into living, breathing works of art, the premise remains the same. Does it make sense for us to tell the master Artist, who sculpted us from nothing, how to best fashion our bodies and our lives?

Yes, God wants us to be honest with Him. He wants to know what we think and feel. But there's a difference in sharing with Him what's on our heart and telling Him how to do His job. When we feel angry or impatient over what we have no control over, it's time to consider the character of God. Contemplate the breadth of His wisdom, the scope of His power, and depth of His love. Remember, He's not only the Almighty God, but our tender, compassionate Father—the one who knows us best and knows what is best for us.

Whether therefore
ye eat, or drink,
or whatsoever ye do,
do all to the
glory
of God.

1 Corinthians 10:31

Good, Better or Best?

We tend to view God as a big picture kind of guy. We know He cares about Ten Commandment kind of stuff, like being faithful to our spouse and refusing to lie, cheat, steal or commit murder. But what we ate for breakfast? That seems a little persnickety, doesn't it?

Contrary to popular belief, God isn't a celestial law enforcement officer. He's a concerned parent. Every rule He makes is to protect us, to add joy and peace to our lives, and to help us grow up to be more like Him. And as every parent knows, the little things matter. Cleaning your room teaches you responsibility and how to care for the possessions you've so graciously been given. Getting enough sleep helps keep you healthy. Eating a nutritious breakfast gets your brain and energy level off to a good start in the morning.

In the same way, the little decisions we make throughout the day, such as what to eat or drink, really do affect the big picture of our lives. The choices we make, both big and small, either bring honor and glory to God by doing what pleases Him (and is ultimately best for us) or they glorify our own self-centered (and in the long run, destructive) inclinations and whims.

Everything we do...every bite we take, every word we speak, every purchase we make at the mall...matters. That's one reason why staying close to God in prayer throughout the day is so important. The closer we are to Him, the more clearly we will hear His voice, and the more easily we will be able to discern not just between good and bad, but between good, better and best.

Greater love
hath no man than this,
that a man lay down
his life for his
friends.

John 15:13

Put Your Life on the Line

What is your most valuable possession? Your life. To give that away, willingly, to save the life of another shows a depth of love unequaled by any other kind of sacrifice. Thankfully, very few of us will ever find ourselves in a position that would require such a costly example of true love. But Jesus did. He willingly offered His life to bridge the divide that our rebellion cut between us and God.

Rebellion sounds like a pretty strong word. But anytime we choose to go our own way, instead of the direction God lays out for us, we turn our back on the One who loves us. Amazingly, it's friends like us, often fickle instead of faithful, for whom Jesus laid down His life.

Even when we don't act like a friend, Jesus still counts us as one. We can hold tightly to that truth simply by remembering what Jesus gave up for us—the ultimate sacrifice. So how can we be a friend to Him in return? We can give up our lives in a different way. We can lay down our time, our treasures, our talents, our desires and our future, as a Thank You gift to God. Even then, we can't out-give or out-love God. He takes the life we offer Him and in return gives us one that is richer, deeper and more abundant than we had before—one that even extends beyond death.

"What a friend we have in Jesus..." The lyrics of that old hymn should be our theme song, a chorus we can sing with confidence and joy every day of our lives.

But they that wait
upon the Lord shall
renew their strength;
they shall mount up
with wings as eagles;
they shall run,
and not be weary;
and they shall walk,
and not faint.

Isaiah 40:31

God's Gym

If you want to increase your strength, you go to the gym. You strain your muscles enough to tax them, let them rest, and then repeat. Unfortunately, one trip to the gym isn't enough to produce results. You need to work out consistently. This involves motivation, hard work, and a bit of discomfort. But the result is certain. Eventually you'll grow stronger. If you stop working out, the result is just as predictable. You will lose muscle mass.

Building inner strength follows the same kind of repetitive pattern. When we're in the middle of a crisis and feeling mentally, physically, or emotionally fragile or fatigued, the doors of God's gym are always open, inviting us into His presence to help renew our strength.

Instead of swinging a kettle bell or running on a treadmill, we grow stronger by learning to wait on God. That sounds pretty easy, like sitting at a movie theatre with a big tub of popcorn waiting for the feature film to start. But waiting on God isn't passive, it's active. It means resisting the temptation to try to make everything work out the way we want it to in our own timing and in our own strength. It means turning to God over and over again, allowing Him to strengthen weak areas of our character and stretch us in ways we didn't know we could bend. It means doing the right thing at the right time, even if it feels uncomfortable or a little bit scary.

The more we choose to wait on God, the less we'll feel as though it's our job to carry the weight of the world upon our shoulders. As God renews our inner strength, we'll find our faith growing stronger at the very same time.

To every thing there is a season.

Ecclesiastes 3:1

Change Is In the Wind

Every season has its beauty and its challenges. Summer has long, sunny days—and bugs. Fall has the brief beauty of autumn leaves—followed by barren branches, as another growing season comes to an end. Winter has ice skating—and scraping ice off car windshields. Spring has buds beginning to bloom—and mud.

The seasons of our lives follow suit: infancy, childhood, adolescence, early adulthood, maturity and beyond. Each has its joys and its challenges, as we welcome in something new and leave something behind. This cycle of change actually helps our gratitude grow. It reminds us we can't take anything for granted, because change is inevitable. When we're in a difficult season, it's encouraging to remember that this too will end. And when we're beginning something new and exciting, knowing that this doesn't come around every day makes us all the more grateful for what we're experiencing right now.

Everything has a beginning and an end, except God. And thanks to His love for us, although we had a beginning, we will join Him in celebrating an eternity that has no end. Our bodies may return to dust, but there's more that awaits us—another season of change. Just like nature, these changing seasons are necessary for our growth. What are you saying "good-bye" and "hello" to in the current season you're in? Take a moment to celebrate this fleeting period of life.

Knowing it won't come again may feel a bit bittersweet, but God promises that what lies ahead will be even greater than what we've left behind.

I have overcome the world.

John 16:33

Acorns May Fall...

Remember the story of Chicken Little? An acorn falls on the head of a perpetually pessimistic chick who instantly jumps to the conclusion that the sky is falling! This folk tale, also known as Henny Penny, was repeated orally for hundreds of years before it first came out in print in the early 1800s. Obviously, people have been able to relate to this "sky is falling" mentality for centuries.

Do you lean more toward a Chicken Little, or a John 16:33, outlook on life? This verse in the Gospel of John isn't encouraging us to don rose-colored glasses or a pair of blinders when we read the morning paper or encounter trouble in our own personal lives. It clearly states that acorns will fall. And we shouldn't be surprised when they happen to fall on our own unsuspecting heads. But, unlike Chicken Little, we also shouldn't let that send us into a spiral of melancholy. The story isn't over yet.

For God, the future is His-story. The ending is already written. And it's a happy one. Yes, along the way there will be trouble. Jesus, who is the one telling us to "be of good cheer" certainly encountered plenty. He never minimized the tribulation, but instead, He focused on the bigger picture—His Father was at work behind the scene.

Let's just say "no" to following in the footsteps of pessimistic poultry. Instead, let's rely on the words, the experience, and the promises of Jesus.

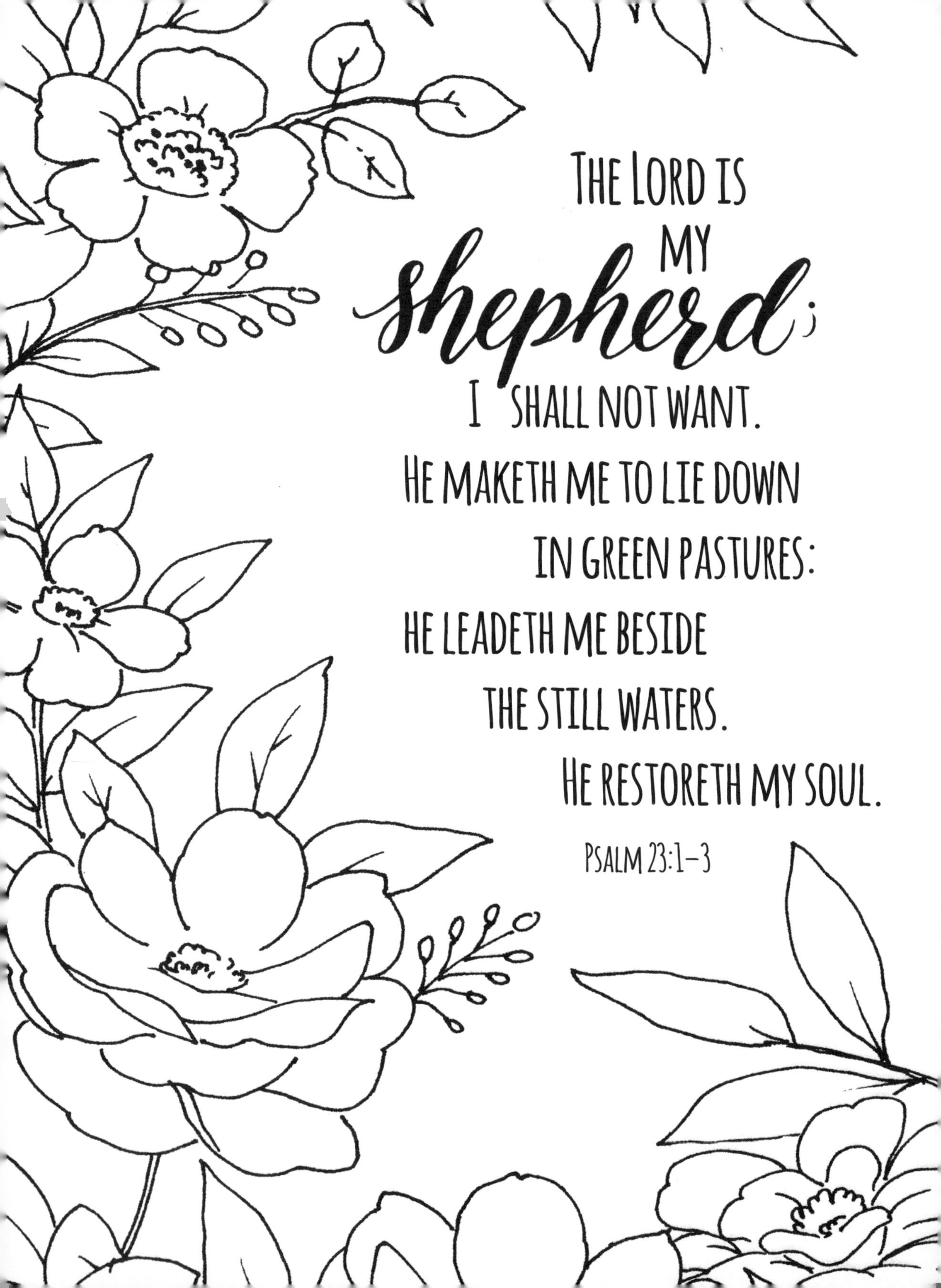
The Lord is
my
shepherd;
I shall not want.
He maketh me to lie down
in green pastures:
he leadeth me beside
the still waters.
He restoreth my soul.
Psalm 23:1–3

Step Away From the Flock

Sheep get a bad rap. People joke about them being rather dim-witted, but it's isn't true. They're fairly intelligent when it comes to the barnyard community. However, they have a few tendencies that promote this perception. First, they frighten easily—which is one reason why they flock together. Secondly, they often follow the flock, even if the flock is headed the wrong direction. Once again, this isn't because they're stupid. It circles back to reason one. They stick with the flock because it's safer. Third, sheep have an amazing memory for faces. They recognize the individual sheep in their flock—as well as the face of their shepherd.

The Bible refers to Jesus as our Good Shepherd. Have we spent enough time with Him to recognize Him? Like sheep, we may feel safe hanging out with the crowd and following whatever they do. It's comfortable to fit in. But sometimes, the flock isn't headed the right direction. We need to take our eyes off the rest of the sheep and put them back on our Shepherd to make certain we're headed toward what we truly need: security, refreshment, rest, and revival.

The rest of the flock may try to convince us we can restore ourselves after a hard week by ordering just one more glass of wine, indulging in a spending spree at the mall, or watching a movie that celebrates things that make us a bit uncomfortable. These may provide a momentary rush that feels like revival. But it doesn't last. We actually feel worse soon afterwards.

The restoration Jesus offers runs soul-deep. It fills the deepest part of us with what truly satisfies, gifts like peace, purpose, and contentment. Be a sheep in the very best sense. Remember your Shepherd and choose to follow wherever He leads.

Give and it shall be given unto you...

Luke 6:38

A God-Sized Portion

Some believe it's the real motive behind "paying it forward." But God's Word is the true source behind the powerful concept that what we give, we'll receive in kind.

As Luke 6:38 niv continues, it provides a mental picture of an overflowing measuring cup, where "a good measure, pressed down, shaken together and running over, will be poured into your lap. For with the measure you use, it will be measured to you." That doesn't mean we should give to get. 2 Corinthians 9:7 says, "God loveth a cheerful giver," not a giver with a self-serving, ulterior motive.

When we give—whether it's our time, our money, or our resources—it should be without the expectation of getting anything in return. However, God's Words should spur us on toward greater generosity, driven more by the prompting of His Spirit, than a meticulous assessment of our bank account or daily agenda. With God, our bottom line is much more fluid than our budget may lead us to believe.

Do to *others* as you would have them do to *you.*

Luke 6:31 NIV

The Golden Rule

Even as little kids, if we didn't know the Bible, we still knew the Golden Rule. We heard it from parents and teachers and anyone else who tried to shift our selfish, self-centered behavior toward a more loving, altruistic direction. It was a great lesson, because it made so much sense—even to a five-year-old. "Do you enjoy being hit? Then don't hit!" "Do you like chocolate chip cookies? So does your sister, so share!"

At its heart, the Golden Rule was not only encouraging us toward choosing more loving actions, but teaching us empathy. Picturing someone else walking in our shoes is the first step toward trying their unfamiliar shoes on our own growing feet.

As adults, the Golden Rule is as valid for us today as it was when we were kids. Now, it's God, instead of parents and teachers, reminding us to treat others as we'd like to be treated. Pay attention to how many opportunities you have to apply the Golden Rule today.

COMMIT
TO THE LORD
WHATEVER YOU DO,
AND HE WILL
ESTABLISH
YOUR PLANS.

PROVERBS 16:3 NIV

God's Planning Commission

If you're going to build your own house, you need to have your plans approved. The city wants to make certain you know what you're doing, that you're building in an area that's zoned for individual family homes, and that your new house is designed with "integrity." When it comes to construction, having integrity means that everything lines up and is architecturally and structurally sound.

If that much thought and planning needs to go into building a house, consider what it takes to build a life. God wants to help you build one that will stand against any storms that may come your way, one that is built with integrity—sturdy, straight and true. That's why God asks to be involved in the early planning stages of each and every day. Whether we're making big plans for the future or simply heading out for lunch with a friend, committing what we do to God simply means inviting Him to be part of the planning process.

When we ask for God's guidance and wisdom, with a sincere, attentive heart, He will help us move ahead with our plans in confidence or nudge us toward changing them before we put too much time and effort into a structure that will not stand. God's Spirit often speaks to us through peace or through a nagging sense of unease. One means go, while the other means wait—or even stop and immediately make a U-turn.

The more time we spend in prayer with God, the more familiar we'll be with His voice, and the more frequently we'll find that our plans will begin to reflect our Father's own heart in their scope and purpose.

For
God
so loved the
world,
that he gave his
only begotten Son,
that whosoever
believeth in him
should not perish,
but have
everlasting
life.

John 3:16

Welcome to the Neighborhood

"Jesus loves me, this I know, for the Bible tells me so..." Every Sunday school student knows this song by heart. From Genesis through the book of Revelation, the Bible tells us how much God loves us, evident through His words and His actions, over and over again. Some of us have trouble accepting God's love for us. We're afraid He can't forgive us for something we've done. We're afraid we're simply not remarkable enough to be worthy of God's love. We're afraid news this good can't possibly be true.

Still others of us accept God's love for ourselves whole-heartedly, but have trouble accepting His love for the rest of the world. "Certainly, this can't include (fill-in-the-blank)!" we mutter. "Not that church; not those people!" Yet God makes it clear: He so loved the people of the world that He made a way for every individual to come to Him through faith.

So which side do we tend to lean toward most? Do we have a harder time loving others or ourselves? Neither way reflects the heart of God, a heart that loves us so much that He considered our life on earth too short a time to spend together. That's why His love, and our lives, extend beyond the grave and into eternity.

Whether we are the ones who feel inferior, or we have a mental list of those we feel God should bar from the pearly gates, our beliefs don't match up with God's truth. If we're going to be spending eternity together, let's ask God to help us get comfortable getting to know and love ourselves and our neighbors the way He does—right here and now.

As for me and my house, we will serve the Lord.
Joshua 24:15

Behind Closed Doors

Home is where we can let it all hang out. No make-up, no problem. Sweats and a tee shirt or pjs and slippers? Perfectly acceptable for an evening in. If a few dust bunnies or piles of laundry happen to be hanging out with us, there's no cause for concern. After all, this is the one place we can be ourselves, empty pizza boxes and all.

There's nothing wrong with being casual and relaxed in our own house. But sometimes we get so comfortable that we take what we own, and who we love, for granted. That includes God. There are more ways to serve God at home as a family than by saying grace before meals, taping a Scripture verse to the kids' bathroom mirror, or displaying a dusty family Bible on the coffee table. One of the best ways is to treat each other with love and respect.

It's amazing how we often treat the people we know best, and profess to love the most, with less regard than we would a business client. It's been said that "familiarity breeds contempt." We believe we'd never let it go that far, yet how often do we allow familiarity to breed annoyance, selfishness, or sarcasm?

One way we can honor God as a family is by honoring those He's given us as family, whether they are our children, our parents, or our spouse. The way we treat each other as family behind closed doors will be evident when we're outside in the world. Love and respect isn't something we can turn off and on. They're either present or they're not. And when they're present, our family can become one of the most powerful messages preached in the world today, without even saying a word.

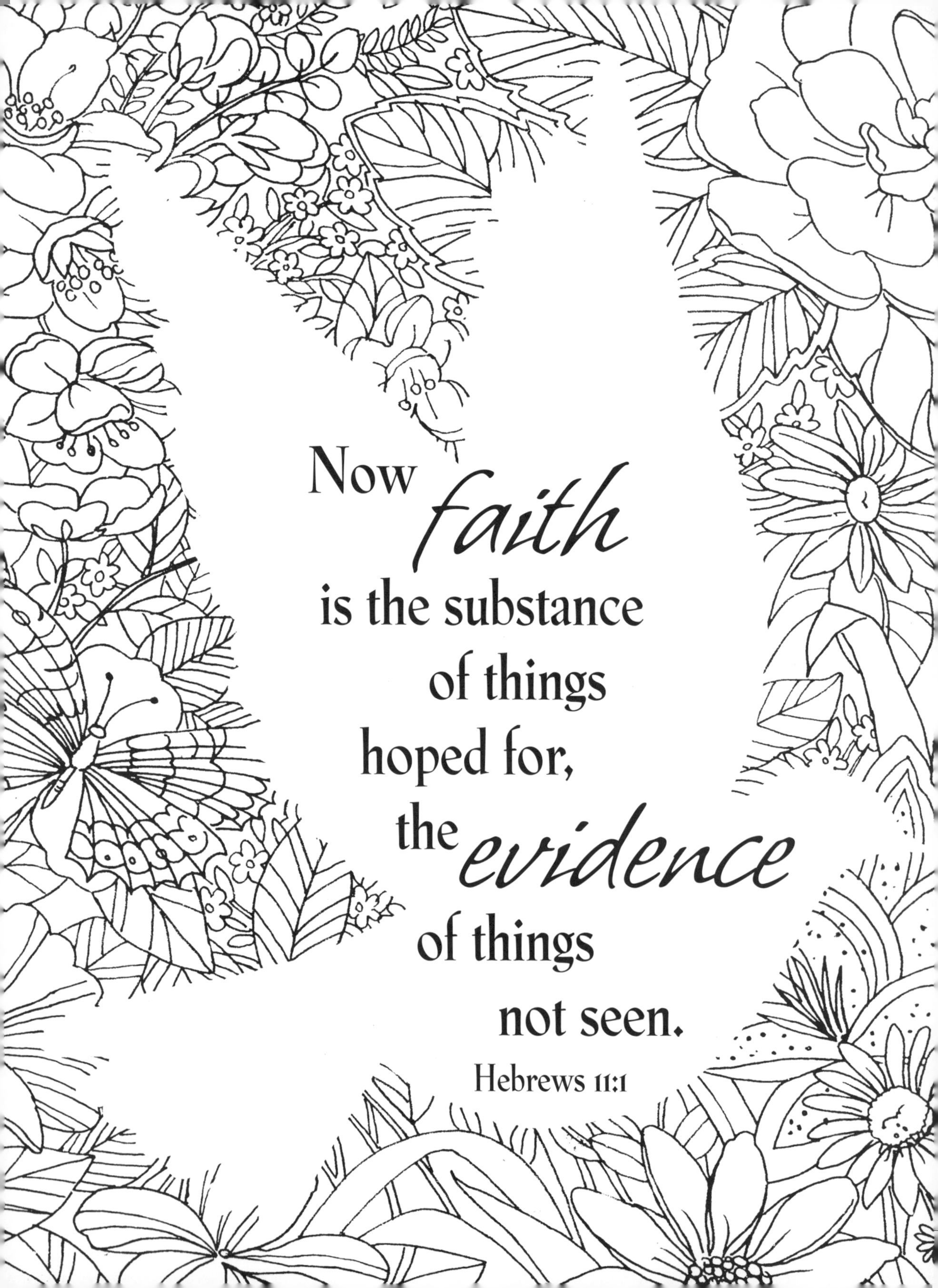

Now *faith*
is the substance
of things
hoped for,
the *evidence*
of things
not seen.

Hebrews 11:1

A Faithful Friend

If a good friend promises to meet you for lunch at your favorite restaurant in ten minutes, you hop in the car and head that direction. You don't have an internal debate over whether or not she will show. If you have faith in her word, her character, and her track record of dependability in the past, it's a no-brainer. You simply take her at her word and go. You don't have concrete "proof" she's going to show. You simply believe she will.

At the beginning, every relationship takes a little "leap of faith." The first time you meet someone, you may not know anything about this person. Or maybe you've heard a bit about her from a mutual acquaintance: "You simply have to meet her! I think you two will really hit it off!" As you spend more time together, your faith in that person has the chance to grow.

The same holds true with God. Whether you're new to the relationship or not, your faith in God will grow as time goes by. Want a stronger faith? You don't acquire it by trying harder to believe or trusting God for things He's never promised to provide. True faith grows stronger as we spend more time with God.

We do that by inviting Him to join us as we make decisions and interact with others throughout the day. We can also learn more about how our invisible, almighty Father relates to people by reading their true life stories in the Bible. We may not be able to see God, but we can see evidence of His loving hand at work in our own lives and throughout history.

Come unto me,

ALL YE THAT LABOUR

AND ARE HEAVY LADEN,

AND I WILL GIVE YOU REST.

MATTHEW 11:28

Good and Rested

A good night's sleep is a wonderful thing. But Jesus isn't talking about getting enough beauty sleep in this verse. He isn't even talking about taking time out for a much-needed vacation. He's actually talking about how He provides rest for our souls.

So, what does a rested soul look like? Let's start by picturing a weary soul, bone-tired from trying to do what's right—in our own strength. You know what that feels like. You try so hard to be a great wife and mother, then berate yourself when you lose your temper or feel annoyed with, instead of grateful for, your spouse or your kids. You know a friend is hurting and you try to do everything you can to be what she needs, but she needs more than you can give. Every time they ask for volunteers at church or in your community, you raise your hand, because you know you are able to do that job, without bothering to ask God if you should do that job.

A heart that loves God is a heart that longs to do good. But our time and energy are limited. God never created us to be our family's, our friend's, our church's, or the world's savior. That is His job. We cannot even save ourselves.

That's why we need God's help in finding rest for our souls. We need Him to help us build boundaries into our lives, knowing when to say "yes" and when to say "no." We need Him to help us forgive ourselves when we're imperfect, impatient, yet well-intentioned. We need God to provide us with spiritual rest. For a rested soul is a beautiful thing. It's allure is evident in a godly, balanced life.

I can do
all things
through Christ
which
strengtheneth
me.

Philippians 4:13

Today's the Day

Procrastination is a double-edged sword. On one hand, it feels good to put off something we dread. Maybe the task feels too big or too hard. Maybe it promises to be uncomfortable or embarrassing. Or perhaps we're afraid we'll flat out fail.

Though we may enjoy the temporary reprieve, whatever we put off only seems to grow heavier and harder the longer we refuse to face up to it. Take a bad habit, for instance. The longer we put off that diet, using the gym membership we already paid for, or just saying "no" to spending more than we make each month, the more power we're actually allowing it to have over our lives.

But God's power is bigger and stronger than any obstacle we may face. Best of all, God assures us this same power is at work in us. With Him, we can tackle whatever lies ahead, including anything we wish we could put off until tomorrow—or forever.

What things on your To Do list never seem to get crossed off? Put them on a "I Wish I Never Had To Do" list. Then, each day, ask God to help you cross one thing off that list. It could be a personal matter, like making a difficult phone call, admitting you've made a mistake, or being the first person to make a positive move toward mending a relationship. Maybe it's Day One in a long term commitment, such as starting a diet or scheduling a long overdue doctor's appointment. It can even be something as small as getting the oil changed in your car.

Each morning, ask God to bring to mind anything you keep putting off until tomorrow. Then, with His help, do it today.

Thy word is a lamp
unto my feet,
and a light
unto my path.

Psalm 119:105

Lord, Light My Way

Imagine walking through a dense forest at midnight. There's a new moon, invisible from earth. But even if it were full, the trees towering overhead would block out its light, just as it already has with the stars. You're walking an unfamiliar path, uneven and littered with rocks. It's tempting to wait until sunrise to proceed, but you can't. Whatever you need to do has to be done now. So you fumble your way forward, stumbling on stones, hoping you haven't made a wrong turn. It's hard going and you've no guarantee you'll end up where you want to go.

Now, picture the same scene with a powerful flashlight in your hand. It may not turn night to day, but with that one bright beam you can see far enough ahead of you to accurately navigate the path. Your journey is not only faster, but safer, and undoubtedly more pleasant.

That's what God's Word can do for your life. The Bible is not a map, or even a guidebook. It's more like a love letter written by a Father who longs for you to know Him better. Through letters, history, poetry, prophecy, and eyewitness accounts, the Bible illuminates who God is, who we are, and what we mean to Him. It shines a light of truth that helps us differentiate between good and evil. It points out the way that will lead us toward drawing closer to God, closer to others, and closer to living up to our potential in this life.

It doesn't light up the whole forest. We will still live with plenty of questions and mystery in this life. But the light of God's Word will provide safe passage as we make our way forward along the path that lies ahead of us today.

A friend loveth at all times.

Proverbs 17:17

All-Weather Friendships

We get to choose our friends. You'd think that would make it easy to love them at all times. But we are complex individuals. What you see isn't always what you get! And the longer we know each other, the more at home we feel, and the more "real" we become in each other's presence—for better or for worse.

Loving our friends can be tough when they act, well...just like us—like flawed, emotional, human beings. But that's where true love comes in. Love doesn't just hang around when the going is easy. Love is here for the long haul, through life's ups and downs, hormones, bad hair days, victory and defeat.

So, how do we love well? With a balance of truth and grace. We extend our real, authentic selves to our friends and invite them to do the same. We challenge each other to live up to our God-given potential, even if that means voicing an uncomfortable truth, now and again. When those occasions arise, we broach tough subjects with tenderness, humility, grace, and prayer. And if we happen to be the one who's being challenged, we respond with those same attributes.

Over the years, across the miles, from mountaintop highs to Death Valley lows, through sunny days, as well as showers, traveling the road of life with a sincere circle of friends is one of the greatest blessings we can receive. It's not only where we can experience the joy of feeling loved, but learn some of the ins and outs of loving others well.

He Careth for You.

1 Peter 5:7

Cherished Child

You are precious to God. How do you handle something precious? You cherish it. That means more than simply holding it in high regard. Being fully aware of its value, you devote yourself to protecting it and caring for it to the best of your ability. That's God's plan for you, His beloved.

That means anxiety really has no place in your life. Sure, it will tug at your heart, your head, and your stomach now and then. But instead of letting it drag you down with it, lift it up and hand it over to God. That's the only productive thing that can come from anxious thoughts. Turn every worry into a prayer, putting it straight into God's hands and removing it from your own.

The more aware you become of how much you mean to God, the less anxious you'll find you feel. To that end, may you come to know the peace of His presence, the security of His faithfulness, the hope of His promises, the joy of His blessing, and the comfort of His tender, eternal love through prayer and spending time in His arms. May this knowledge give you the confidence to live the life He's set before you to the fullest—and to share the grace and lovingkindness He's so graciously bestowed on you with everyone who crosses your path.

In all thy ways
acknowledge him,
and he shall
direct thy paths.
Proverbs 3:6

Take the First Step

Would you take a stroll on the Grand Canyon Skywalk? This four-inch thick, clear glass walkway extends 70 feet out over the Canyon and offers a unique view—4,000 feet straight down to the Colorado River. The highest manmade structure in the world, the Skyway exceeds engineering requirements by 400% and is able to support the weight of 70 fully-loaded Boeing 747 airplanes. But would you trust it to support you?

Fears and phobias aside, your answer illustrates the difference between faith and trust. Faith is a noun; it's something you have. You may have faith in the integrity of the builders and believe their design and materials are sound. But it's trust (which is a verb) that enables you to take that first step.

We may believe God exists. We may believe that He loves us, forgives us, and hears our prayers. But if our belief doesn't impact how we live our lives, we don't really trust Him. We may argue that we need to understand Him more fully before we step out of our comfort zone. But the truth is, our finite minds will never be able to fully comprehend an infinite God.

We don't have to understand the principles of physics and engineering that keep the Skyway in the sky, if we trust that those who built it do. The same is true of God. If we believe He can see the best path for us, we can choose to trust God to lead us down it. Through prayer, reading the Bible, and listening to the wise counsel of others who trust in God, our heavenly Father will direct our path. As we trust Him day by day, we'll move forward step by step.

Because of the
Lord's great love
we are not consumed,
for his compassions
never fail.
They are new
every morning;
great is your
faithfulness.

Lamentations 3:22-23 NIV

Begin Again

The first blank page in a new journal...freshly tilled earth, ready for planting to begin...the beach after the tide has receded, but before any footsteps have appeared on the sand...the first breath of a newborn, fresh from her mother's womb.... There's something pure and exhilarating about the promise of a fresh start. Mistakes, regrets, and what's happened in the past have no place here. All that lies ahead is possibility and potential.

That's how God sees us each morning as we open our eyes. His love for us is so perfectly unconditional, His forgiveness so all-inclusive, and His faithfulness so rock solid that our yesterdays do not have the power to blemish today. At least, from God's point of view. We may still feel its consequences, but our past does not determine the trajectory of our life. This moment, right here and right now, is all we have the power to shape and transform. And with God's help, the possibilities for this moment are limitless.

Regardless of the choices we make, God's compassion for us never wears thin, like an old, threadbare quilt. Instead, it's like a blanket that's constantly being rewoven from the softest, warmest, purest fibers, covering us completely. Every night, let's picture ourselves being safely swaddled in a blanket of God's flawless compassion. Then, each morning we can imagine ourselves emerging fresh and new into the promise of a new day, an experience akin to that of a butterfly emerging from a cocoon. Just as God's compassions are continually new, thanks to God, so are we.

God is not the author of confusion, but of peace.

1 Corinthians 14:33

The Peace Process

Anxious? Confused? Uncertain of where to turn? Turn to God. He has the wisdom and power to help you untangle whatever mess life has laid out in front of you. Like a fine chain, twisted into what appears to be an unsalvageable muddle, there is a solution. But it will take time, and patience, to get the knots untied.

In the meantime, don't allow your mind to get twisted up in the process. God promises peace amidst chaos and clarity in place of confusion. When you start to feel your body getting tenser, your mind racing faster, and your heart sinking lower, take a moment to reconnect with God. Close your eyes and simply breathe. Ask God to calm your anxious thoughts and replace your stress with trust. Allow Him to reveal the next step you need to take. Just focus on that one—and get it done. Then, if need be, take another time out to breathe and pray.

Slowly, but surely, God can help you sort out a jumbled mess of any size and circumstance. Just remember that an oasis of peace is within reach whenever confusion tries to creep back in.

THOU SHALT LOVE THY *neighbour* AS THYSELF.

MATTHEW 22:39

I See You

When you're hungry, you grab a snack. When you're tired, you head to bed. When you're cold, you put on a sweater. When it comes to taking care of ourselves, it's second nature to do what we can to make sure our needs are met. That's love in action.

Loving our neighbor takes a bit more forethought. It's hard to meet someone else's needs if we don't know what they are. Love pays attention. It doesn't look past people, it looks at them. It takes time to listen and ask questions. It strives to see others from God's point of view, knowing they are worthy of respect, patience, and care. And when our neighbors are difficult to get along with or hard to read when it comes to figuring out what they need, love prays. A lot.

Begin every morning by asking God to open your eyes to those you'll encounter during the day, not only so you'll see them more clearly as individuals, but that you'll be sensitive to better understanding their needs—and knowing how to best reach out and meet them in a way that best reflects God's love.

LET US NOT BECOME WEARY IN
doing good,
FOR AT THE PROPER TIME
WE WILL REAP A HARVEST
IF WE DO NOT GIVE UP.

GALATIANS 6:9 NIV

Signs of Life

Imagine a farmer meticulously planting corn in his field. In a few weeks, he races down to the furrows of newly turned earth with great anticipation. Then his face falls. It looks exactly the same as it did before—like nothing more than dirt. Discouraged, and even a bit angry, he heads back to the farmhouse to break the news to his wife: "No corn on the cob tonight!"

Ridiculous, right? Everyone knows that plants take time to reach maturity. So do the seeds of good deeds. Whether it's being consistent in our love and discipline of our children, treating a caustic co-worker with respect, or sharing God's message of love with a neighbor, we can't expect to see results overnight. Doing so only leads to disappointment. It may even lead us to give up on something that's destined to be fruitful—just not quite yet.

Growth of any kind takes time. When it comes to doing the right thing in a difficult situation, it can be hard to hang in there for the long haul. But God continues to give us the gift of a new day. Every evening, we need to thank Him for the strength to do what He's called us to do. The next morning we forget what's behind us and pray for the strength to do what needs to be done today. Even if we don't see any change, we can be encouraged knowing God's hand is at work right alongside us, carefully tending the soil in any and every situation. All that's left for us to do is keep our eyes open, looking for the first little signs of life.

O TASTE
AND SEE
THAT THE
LORD
IS GOOD.

PSALM 34:8

Soul Food

"Try a bite...you'll like it!" Probably every mother since the dawn of time has uttered a phrase similar to this to a child who's turned his or her head away from a perfectly good, healthy, tasty meal. As adults, hopefully our tastebuds, and our willingness to trying something new, has matured a bit. But regardless of our age, there are times when our own stubbornness and childishness can still rob us of trying something good.

Take God, for instance. To get to know Him, we have to get close enough to "taste" Him. We need to give prayer, reading the Bible, becoming involved in a church, and moving forward in faith each day a try. The more ways we find to connect with God in our lives, the more we'll recognize and appreciate His goodness.

How can you "taste and see" God's goodness today? Spend time pondering the words of Psalm 34:8. You could also take your Bible and read Psalm 34 in its entirety. Pray for insight into what this portion of Scripture means. Ask God to help you better understand how good He is to you through experiences in your own life. Take time to thank Him for the blessings you receive today. Consider starting a Blessings Book, where you spend a few moments at the beginning or end of each day to write down how you've experienced God's goodness firsthand. Pray without asking for anything, simply thank God for who He is to you and to the world. Enjoy a meal in silence, really tasting every bite—as you thank God for the gift of food, the kind that nourishes our body, as well as the kind that nourishes our soul.

And what does the Lord require of you?

To act justly
and to love mercy
and to walk humbly
with your God.

Micah 6:8 NIV

Without Reservation

Justice, mercy, and humility all have something in common. We can only practice them in the context of relationship. To "act justly" requires us to be fair and impartial, honorable and honest in our dealings with others. To "love mercy" means that we choose to error on the side of generosity and compassion, readily offering grace and forgiveness—especially when we feel others least deserve it. To "walk humbly" with God means that we see ourselves through God's eyes, as no more or less than He created us to be.

Humility helps us not only see ourselves in proper relationship to God, but to those around us. It lays the groundwork for us to act justly and love mercy. When we're aware of how gracious God has been with us, how we continue to receive more than we deserve, it's easier for us to generously offer that same benevolence to others.

Anytime our heart simmers angrily over feeling we've been treated unjustly or that a situation "isn't fair," all we need to do is look squarely at God. What a wonderful thing it is that God extended mercy to us, instead of clinging to what's fair. Yes, He is just, but He is also merciful. That's the same balance He asks us to attain in our own lives. Through our relationship with God, we're able to have a more godly relationship with others. Through His example, and His power, we have the opportunity to extend true love, a gift that cannot be earned, but is given freely, without reservation.

For I know
the plans
I have for you...
plans to give
you hope and
a future.
Jeremiah 29:11 NIV

Make Yourself at Home

The prophet Jeremiah delivered this powerful message from God to the people who were currently living in exile in Babylon. All they really wanted was to go home, to go back to what they knew, the land they loved, the style of life they'd become accustomed to. But God had a better plan.

The rest of the story, written in chapter 29 in the book of Jeremiah, explains that God tells His people to settle in for the long haul. He tells them to build houses, get married, work toward peace and prosperity right where they are: in Babylon. He promises He will bring them home—70 years from now. That means many of those in exile wouldn't live to see this promise fulfilled.

That's not quite the hope and future we want God to promise us. When we're in the midst of difficult circumstances, we want God to act NOW. We want our future to begin today. And it does. But part of that future may mean settling in and making ourselves at home right where we are, even if it feels as though we're experiencing our own version of exile.

God does have a plan for us, a plan for our good. God wants us to make the most of today, even if today is not what we had planned. By refusing to treat difficult circumstances as simply stepping stones toward something better, God helps us find joy, hope, and purpose right here, right now. He helps us look toward the future without missing out on the gift of today.

BE
strong
AND OF A GOOD
courage...
FOR THE LORD THY
God
IS WITH THEE
WHITHERSOEVER
THOU GOEST.

JOSHUA 1:9

Joy for the Journey

Where are you headed? A new job? A new address? A new stage of life or relationship? Whatever direction you're headed, whether it's a road you want to take or one you have no choice but to travel, you never walk it alone. God is right beside you every step of the way. He's there to strengthen you when you get weary or discouraged, to remind you that you're gifted and resilient, and to whisper how proud He is of how far you've come. He's like a cheerleader, life coach and parent all rolled into one.

But God is more than that. He's your Father, Creator, and Friend. He doesn't stay close to just give you a pep talk or build your confidence. He's near because He wants to be involved in every journey you take, because He loves you—boundlessly, unconditionally, eternally. You are of immeasurable value to Him. No one else could ever fill the unique place you hold in His heart. So, it gives Him great joy to protect you, guide you, and lavish you with His love every day, wherever you are in life. He wants to walk you all the way home to Him, when that day arrives where you can fully understand what it means to walk with Him forever.

Today is just one small part of that journey. But He's right there, next to you, closer than your next breath, as you're reading these very words. What would you like to say to Him this morning? Go ahead. Share it all. He's listening. Then, after your talk, it's time to walk.

Seek ye first

the kingdom of God,

and his righteousness;

and all these things

shall be added unto you.

Matthew 6:33

Firm Foundation

We spend much of our time building our own little kingdoms. We work hard during the week to be able to afford a nice place to live, to stock our pantry with our favorite food, and to fill our closet with a wardrobe that fits our personality, our lifestyle, our budget, and hopefully, our body. We spend our evenings and weekends taking care of our home, buying more groceries, and washing the clothing we wore during the week. When Monday rolls around, we do it all over again.

How we spend our time is how we spend our lives. Are we spending it on something that lasts? In the Sermon on the Mount, of which Matthew 6:33 is a part, we're reminded that our priorities matter. Are we seeking God (and the things that honor Him) during our busy days or simply seeking to ensure that our own personal kingdom will stand?

Sometimes, faith feels like just another thing on our To Do list: go to church, pray, read a few verses from the Bible...repeat. But God isn't a chore we need to complete. He's a Father who wants a relationship with us, because He loves us. When we look to Him throughout the day—not because we feel obligated to, but because we want to spend time with Him—He reminds us there's more to life than making a living. There's love and joy and hope and peace and grace in abundance. Those are the building blocks of God's kingdom and they provide a solid foundation we can build our lives on, as well.

Love…

ALWAYS PROTECTS,

ALWAYS TRUSTS,

ALWAYS HOPES,

ALWAYS PERSEVERES.

Love never fails.

1 CORINTHIANS 13:6–8 NIV

Love Story

The love stories we live don't always look like they do in the movies. Frankly, they're a lot harder to live out in real life. That's because in God's vocabulary, love is a verb, instead of simply a noun. God encourages us to act in loving ways toward others even when we don't feel that Hollywood surge of affection or passion. In Luke 6:27–28 niv, Jesus even tells us to "Love your enemies, do good to those who hate you, bless those who curse you, pray for those who mistreat you." That certainly doesn't look like love on the silver screen.

God isn't asking us to nurture co-dependence or dysfunction in our relationships. 1 Corinthians 13:4–6 niv explains that, "Love is patient, love is kind. It does not envy, it does not boast, it is not proud. It does not dishonor others, it is not self-seeking, it is not easily angered, it keeps no record of wrongs. Love does not delight in evil but rejoices with the truth."

Truth doesn't close its eyes to bad behavior. It discerns between true, godly love and selfish, controlling behavior. While we don't keep a record of wrongs (by carrying grudges, inciting gossip, or withholding love from those who we feel don't deserve it), we are wise in how we love. Sometimes, love cares for others best from a safe distance.

So, how does your love measure up? Without God, a 1 Corinthians 13 kind of love is impossible. But with God, it's the greatest gift we can bestow on those God's put into our lives. The more we allow God to change our hearts, the more our actions change right along with it—including the kind of love story we're writing with our lives today.

He hath
made
every thing
beautiful
in his
time.

Ecclesiastes 3:11

Changing Beauty

The culture in which we live has a narrow definition of beauty. It celebrates youth, a thin frame, and symmetrical features. But individuals are as varied in physical appearance as the natural world. We consider a sunset beautiful, as well as a wild stallion, a hummingbird, autumn leaves, or the tiniest of wildflowers. Diversity is a given in nature. As part of God's art gallery of creation, it's also a given in us.

God has woven intrinsic beauty into each of us, into our physical frame, into our unique personalities and histories, and into the unique place we fill in this world. That beauty is evident throughout our lives, but shows up in different ways with each passing season. Some areas of our lives simply take time to mature. Others may feel like an endless struggle, until the day God reveals a trace of unforeseen goodness and grace. Like the multiple facets of a cut gem, there are so many ways in which our lives can shine.

To become more aware of this beauty in ourselves, and in the lives of those around us, takes both patience and perspective. But if we search for it, we'll find it. After all, God's image is reflected in all of us. It may be dimmed by a person's selfishness or choices in life, but nothing can extinguish it.

Consider every day a treasure hunt, a chance to search for glimpses of His glory. We shouldn't be surprised if we find it in the most unexpected places. After all, the brilliance of autumn leaves shines brightest as they're preparing to fall from the tree. Contrary to what fashion magazines might have us believe, beauty often grows richer as time goes by.

The Lord
is close to the
brokenhearted
and saves those
who are crushed
in spirit.
Psalm 34:18 NIV

An Anchor in Your Storm

There are times when there are no words that can express the depth of your sorrow. There is no loved one whose presence can adequately fill the emptiness you feel. There is no diversion great enough to make you forget. There is no opportunity to turn back the clock. There are times when you know you'll never be the same person you were before.

During those times, God aches right along with you. He's close enough to hear what you cannot say. And He is the only one who is able to take the pieces of your broken heart and tenderly put them back together again. It's true, your heart may never quite look, or feel, the way it did before. But like a mosaic made from broken stones, it can be whole again, recreated in a beautiful new way.

During those dark days, when time itself seems to stand still for you while the rest of the world goes on as though nothing has changed, know that God is near. You may not always feel His presence. Sometimes, pain is so intense that it even seems to overshadow the great I AM. But our feelings don't always tell the truth. God is close, whether we feel His love and comfort at this moment or not. Hold onto that truth. Let it anchor you to the solid ground of His devotion to you, and to His ability to take what looks hopeless and reveal a new path, a new plan, and a new purpose, no matter how great the storm.

If ye have faith

as a grain

of mustard seed...

nothing shall

be impossible unto you.

Matthew 17:20

Think Small

God is so big that our minds cannot fully comprehend Him. And we are so, well…finite. All we need to do is look down over the edge of the Grand Canyon or up into the star-filled night sky to feel rather small. And sometimes, we associate small with insignificant.

But God reassures us that small things can still make a mighty impact on this world. Take a young shepherd boy named David. No one would have picked him as the champion who would fell a nine-foot-tall warrior named Goliath. No one, but God. God knew that David had more than a slingshot and a smooth stone at his disposal. He had faith.

David believed someone needed to stand up to this man who kept making fun of God. Since no one else would, David felt he was the man, or boy, for the job. So in faith, David accepted Goliath's challenge. God honored David's faith by fighting right alongside the young boy who would one day become king of Israel. Together they slew a giant.

Are there any giants in your life God is calling you to face? Whatever God asks you to do, He'll provide what you need to enable you to do it. With an itty-bitty, mustard seed-sized grain of faith, believe what God's promised. Then, step up to the challenge, knowing that you're never too small when God is on your side.

THE Lord BLESS THEE, AND KEEP thee.

NUMBERS 6:24